The Moon

Lesley Sims

Watts Books
London • New York • Sydney

© 1993 Watts Books

Watts Books
96 Leonard Street
London EC2A 4RH

Franklin Watts Australia
14 Mars Road
Lane Cove
NSW 2066

UK ISBN: 0 7496 1029 8

10 9 8 7 6 5 4 3 2 1

Series editor: Pippa Pollard
Editor: Felicity Trotman
Design: Shaun Barlow
Cover design: Edward Kinsey
Artwork: Michael Lye
Cover artwork: Hugh Dixon
Picture research: Ambreen Husain

Educational advisor: Joy Richardson

A CIP catalogue record for this book
is available from the British Library

Printed in Italy by G. Canale & C. SpA

Contents

What is the Moon?

The Moon is a ball of rock, spinning in space. It is about 380,000 kilometres from the Earth. The Moon is a **satellite** of the Earth. A satellite is any object which travels around another. The Moon takes about one month to travel around the Earth. The continuous journey of the Moon around the Earth is called an **orbit.**

▽ The Moon at night seen from the Earth.

The Moon at night

The Moon does not give out light. It shines because it is reflecting the light of the Sun. The Moon is shaped like a ball, but if you watch the Moon for a month, it will seem to change shape. This is because, as the Moon orbits the Earth, the Sun lights up different parts of the side we are looking at. The different shapes we can see are called **phases**.

▷ Moonlight bathes the Earth in a silvery glow.

▽ The Moon orbiting the Earth.

4

The phases of the Moon

When the Moon is between the Sun and the Earth, it is usually invisible to us. The Sun lights up the side away from the Earth. This is a new moon. As the Moon continues its journey, more of it shows each night. When the Moon has travelled half way around the Earth, the whole side facing the Earth is lit. This is a full moon. Then it shrinks to a new moon again.

▷ A crescent moon.

Crescent   First quarter   Gibbous moon   Full moon

Gibbous moon   Last quarter   Crescent

◁ Between new
moon and full moon,
the Moon is waxing.
From full moon back
to new moon, it is
waning.

An eclipse of the Moon

At full moon, the Moon and Sun are on opposite sides of the Earth. Sometimes the Earth gets right between the Sun and the Moon. This blocks the light of the Sun and stops it reaching the Moon. The Earth casts a shadow over the Moon. This is an **eclipse of the Moon.** It happens when the Earth is exactly between the Sun and the Moon, in a straight line.

▷ An eclipse.

▽ Anyone on the night-time side of the Earth can see an eclipse of the Moon when it happens.

Gravity and tides

Gravity is an invisible force which pulls objects together. The Earth's gravity pulls on the Moon. This keeps the Moon in orbit around the Earth. At the same time, the Moon's gravity is pulling on the Earth. It is not strong enough to change the position of the Earth in space. But it does pull on the oceans on the Earth's surface. This is the main cause of the **tides.**

▷ When the tide is out it is low tide. When the tide is in it is high tide.

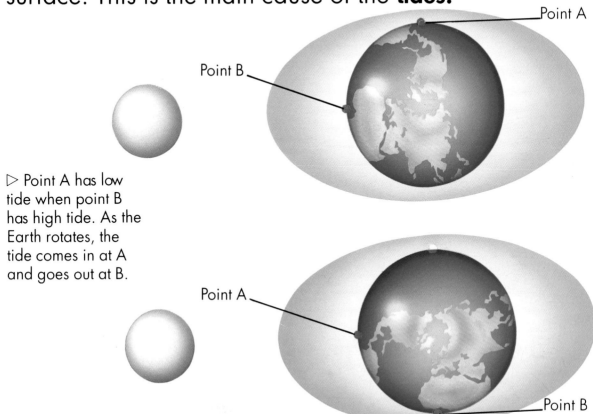

Point A

Point B

▷ Point A has low tide when point B has high tide. As the Earth rotates, the tide comes in at A and goes out at B.

Point A

Point B

11

On the Moon

▷ Even during the day, the Moon's sky is always black.

The Moon is a silent, empty place. There is no air and no water. The Moon's gravity is not strong enough to hold on to them. In places where the Sun shines, it becomes very hot. The temperature reaches more than 100 °C. Away from the Sun, the Moon lies in cold, black shadow. It can be twice as cold as the coldest place on the Earth.

▽ The Moon has a very barren landscape of rock and dust.

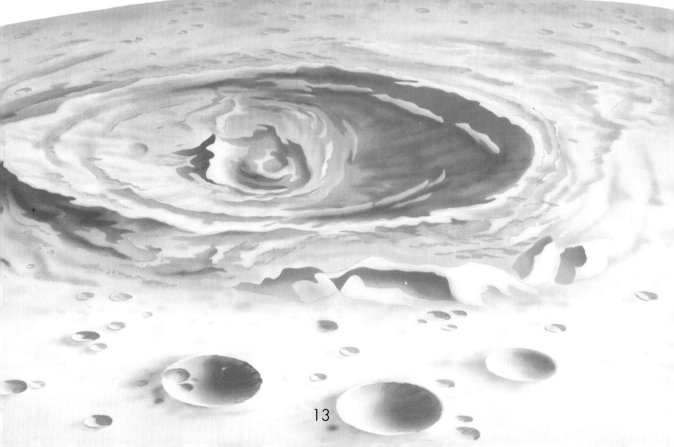

Night and day

We have day and night on Earth because the Earth spins round or **rotates** on its **axis.** The Earth takes 24 hours to rotate once. For some of those hours, one side faces the Sun and it is daytime. As the Earth rotates, that side turns away from the Sun, and for the rest of the 24 hours is in darkness. The Moon takes about a month to rotate.

▽ The side of the Moon which cannot be seen from the Earth is known as the 'far side'.

◁ Day and night on Earth.

▽ The Moon rotates once in the same time it takes to orbit the Earth once, so the same side of the Moon always faces us.

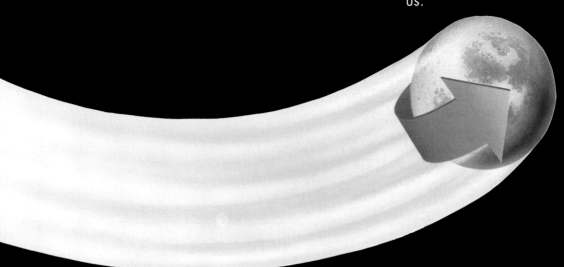

How the Moon was formed

About 4,600 million years ago, the
Earth and Moon formed out of a cloud of
gas and dust whirling around the Sun.
For hundreds of millions of years after
the Moon had formed, space was a
violent place. Lumps of rock often
crashed into the Moon. They made many
of the **craters** which cover the Moon's
surface.

▷ Some of the dark
patches are vast
craters. They filled
up with hot, liquid
rock which
hardened as it
cooled down. They
are called seas
because from the Earth
they look like water.

▽ Specks of dust
stuck together until
they were big
enough to form the
Earth and Moon.

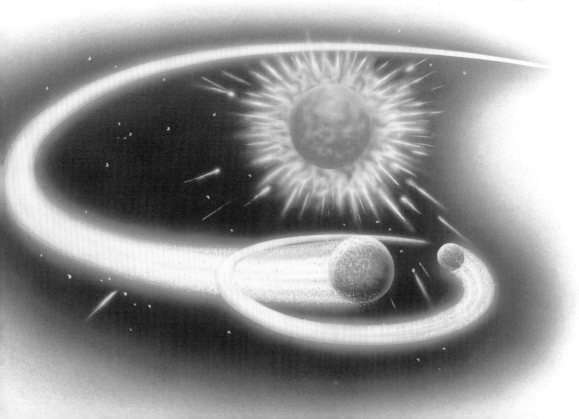

▽ This is how the
Moon may have
looked during its first
one thousand million
years.

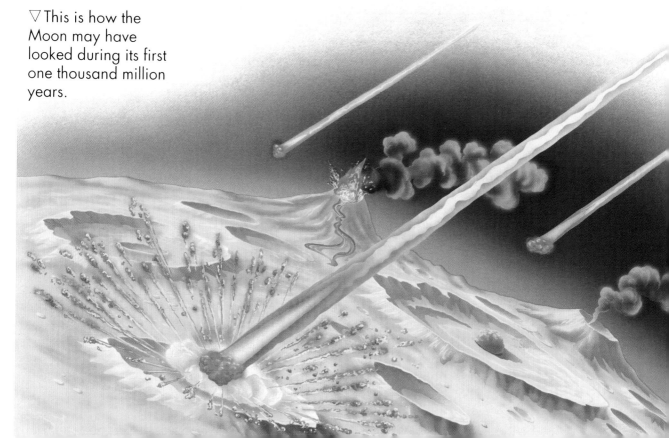

Moon probes

The first close-up pictures of the Moon were taken by orbiters. These were robot spacecraft, or **probes**, which travelled around or past the Moon taking photographs. The Soviet probe Luna 9 was the first to land on the Moon without crashing and being destroyed. America launched five Lunar Orbiters which took photographs of almost the entire Moon.

▽ A picture of the Moon, sent by a Lunar Orbiter.

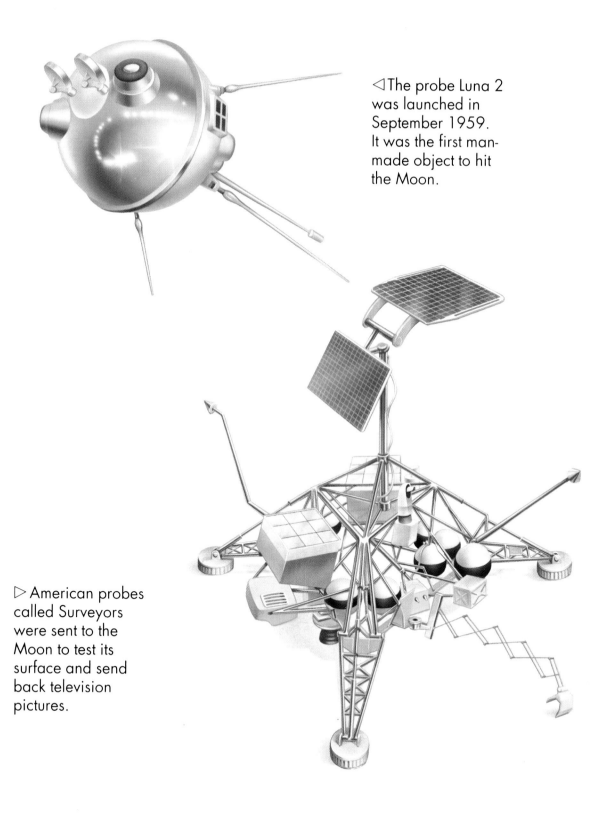

◁ The probe Luna 2 was launched in September 1959. It was the first man-made object to hit the Moon.

▷ American probes called Surveyors were sent to the Moon to test its surface and send back television pictures.

Journey to the Moon

Soviet and American probes showed it was possible for spacecraft to land safely on the Moon. The Americans decided to send **astronauts** to the Moon. They travelled in a spacecraft called Apollo. Inside it was very cramped. The astronauts spent hours practising for the trip. They used models of the spacecraft which did not leave the ground.

▷ The first astronauts about to land on the Moon.

▽ There is no gravity in space. To learn how it feels to be weightless, the astronauts practised under water and in aeroplanes.

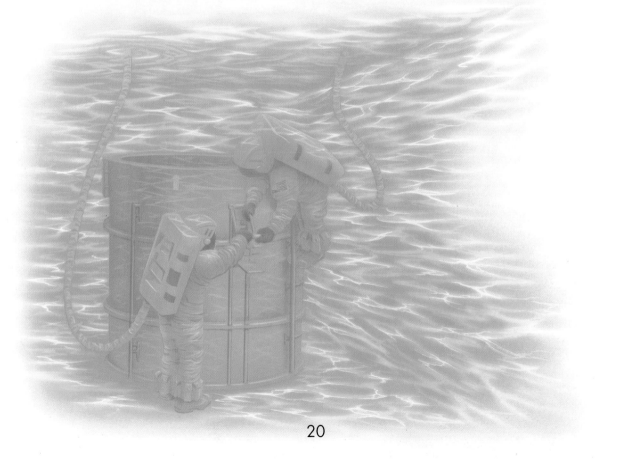

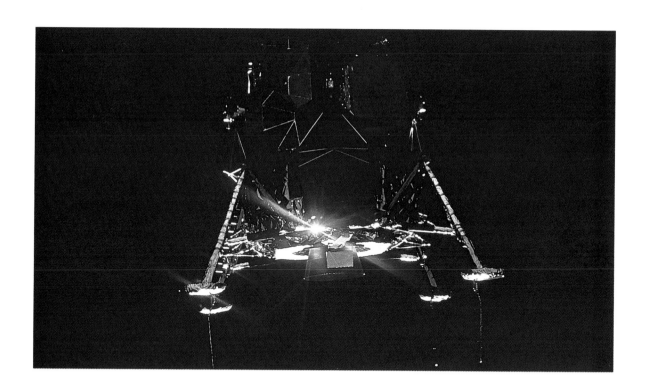

▽ While two
astronauts explored
the Moon, the third
was left in orbit
around it.

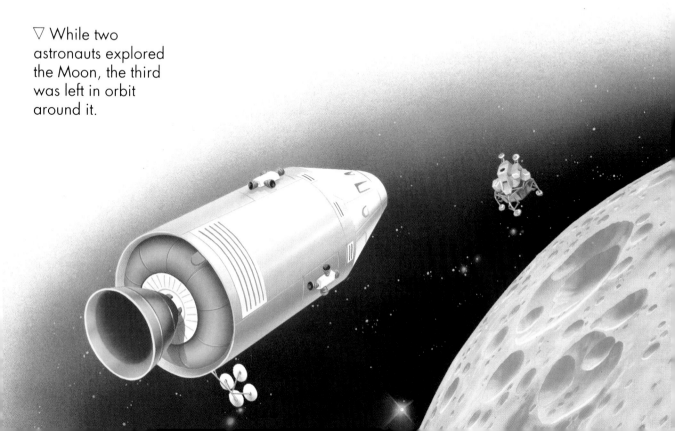

Spacesuits

The astronauts wore special clothes to protect themselves outside the spacecraft. Under the suit was a long vest made of plastic tubes filled with water. This stopped the astronauts from becoming too hot. Their helmets were tinted to protect their eyes. They carried backpacks with oxygen and water. On Earth, the astronauts needed help to get dressed!

▽ The first spacesuits were very bulky.

Undersuit   Trousers

Top of suit

Attaching the backpack

Backpack on   Gloves   22   Helmet   Suited up

Humans on the Moon

The astronauts landed in the Sea of Tranquillity. In their heavy suits, the astronauts found bouncing along was easier than walking. Under their helmets they wore earphones and a microphone, so they could talk to each other, to the **command module** and to scientists on the Earth. Sound cannot travel by itself on the Moon. There is no air to carry it.

▽ Edwin Aldrin climbing down the ladder on the lunar module. Neil Armstrong took this photograph.

◁There is no wind on the Moon to blow the flag. It had wire inside it to make it stick out.

▷ These footprints will be on the Moon for many thousands of years. The Moon has no wind or rain to wash them away.

◁A boulder found by astronauts from Apollo 14.

Mapping the Moon

Between 1959 and 1972, probes, orbiters and the six Moon **missions** learned a huge amount about the Moon. The Soviets sent two remote-controlled vehicles called Lunokhod. Lunokhod 1 travelled over ten kilometres. From the photographs it took, maps could be made for nearly 80,000 square metres of the Moon's surface.

▽ This astronaut is using a television camera to scan the surface of the Moon. Since 1972 no one has landed on the Moon.

Sea of Rain

Sea of Serenity

Ocean of Storms

Archimedes

Kepler

Copernicus

Sea of Tranquillity

Ptolomaeus

Sea of Clouds

Tycho

◁A map of the Moon. The craters are named after famous scientists.

▷The Lunokhod cars were operated from the Earth.

Other moons

The Earth is not the only **planet** to have a satellite **moon.** Mars has two, called Phobos and Deimos. They are both much smaller than our Moon. They are so small, they do not have enough gravity to pull them into a ball shape. Saturn has more than twenty moons. One of them, Titan, is larger than a small planet. Some moons are made of more ice than rock.

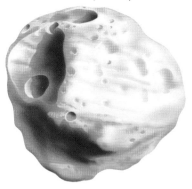

▷ Titania is the largest satellite of Uranus. There seem to be cracks on its surface. These might be caused by water freezing and expanding.

▽ Phobos is a small rocky lump.

△ Callisto, one of Jupiter's moons, is covered in craters.

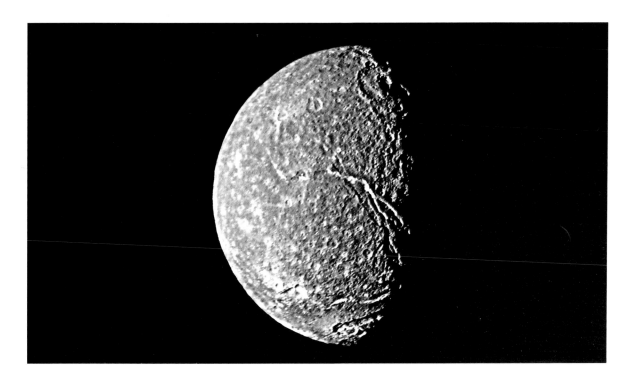

△ Saturn's moon
Enceladus is an ice
satellite. Part of
Enceladus has a
smooth surface.

▷ Titan is so large
that it has an
atmosphere of its
own.

Things to do

- Watch the Moon over a month and keep a record of its phases.

- Model the cratered surface of the Moon in papier mâché or modelling clay.

- Drop a marble into a bowl of flour to see how a crater is formed.

- Make a model of a moon buggy.

Useful addresses:

Junior Astronomical Society,
36 Fairway,
Keyworth,
Nottingham NG12 5DV

British Astronomical Association
Burlington House,
Piccadilly,
London W1V 0NL

Glossary

astronaut Someone who travels in space.

axis An imaginary line which runs through the centre of a planet or moon, around which they spin.

command module The small spacecraft which orbited the Moon, then brought the astronauts back to the Earth.

crater A bowl-shaped hole.

eclipse of the Moon Earth blocking the light of the Sun, causing a shadow to fall over the Moon.

gravity An invisible force which pulls objects together.

mission A space visit.

moon A ball of rock or ice which orbits a planet.

orbit To travel around an object; the continuous journey of one object around another, such as the Moon around the Earth, or the Earth around the Sun.

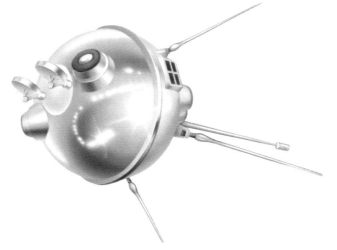

phases The changing shapes of the Moon seen from Earth.

planet A spinning ball of rock or gases and liquids which orbits a star, often orbited by one or more moons.

probe A robot spacecraft.

rotate To spin around.

satellite An object, such as a moon, which orbits another.

tides The movement of the oceans, caused mainly by the pull of the Moon's gravity.

Index

Photographic credits: Chris Fairclough Colour Library 11; Genesis Space Photo Library 13, 14, 18, 26; NASA 17, 21, 25; Science Photo Library (J Sanford) 9, (NASA) 29; TRH Pictures/ NASA 23; ZEFA 3, 5, 7.